YOUR KNOWLEDGE HAS VALUE

- We will publish your bachelor's and
  master's thesis, essays and papers

- Your own eBook and book -
  sold worldwide in all relevant shops

- Earn money with each sale

Upload your text at www.GRIN.com
and publish for free

Bibliographic information published by the German National Library:

The German National Library lists this publication in the National Bibliography; detailed bibliographic data are available on the Internet at http://dnb.dnb.de .

This paper is a polemic pamphlet. The opinion expressed herein is solely the author's own.

Imprint:

Copyright © 2016 GRIN Verlag, Open Publishing GmbH
Print and binding: Books on Demand GmbH, Norderstedt Germany
ISBN: 9783656989042

This book at GRIN:

http://www.grin.com/en/e-book/322938/the-existence-of-god-an-argument-in-favor

Cole Lindsay

The Existence of God. An Argument in Favor

GRIN Publishing

Cole Lindsay

Period 2

Senior Research Paper

The Existence of God

There are hundreds of arguments for and against the case of the existence of God. This topic is very touchy for many scientists, as they might believe that the existence of God would threaten the concrete truths of science, but this is not the case. The existence of God is not only allowed within the realm of science, but it logically fits in to the laws of science that we already have. For these reasons, it is important to conduct research and show the evidence for the argument of the existence of God.

It is imperative to first understand some key terms that will be used in this research, so that there will be minimal confusion as to the meaning of certain ideas. First off, of course, you will need to know the definition of God. God is defined as "The perfect and all-powerful spirit or being that is worshipped especially by Christians, Jews, and Muslims as the one who created and rules the universe" (Grove). Fine-tuning is also a term that is essential to understand for the comprehension of this research. Fine-tune means, "to adjust precisely so as to bring to the highest level of performance or effectiveness" (Grove). In addition, intelligent design is defined as "the theory that matter, the various forms of life, and the world were created by a designing intelligence" (Grove). One field of study that is required to understand is Ontology, which is a belief that "the laws of nature can't be explained without an intelligent mind" (Cartwright 3).

Lastly, a doctrine named Parentheism must be understood to fully grasp the meaning of

this research. Parentheism is defined as "the doctrine that God includes the world as a

part though not the whole of his being" (Grove).

When the topic of morality is brought up, it is hard to get around the fact that

there would be no universal 'right and wrong' if no being were there to set that up in the

first place. Francis Collins shows this when he speaks about his decision early in his life

to become an atheist. "So I became a committed materialist and an obnoxious atheist, and

it sounded very convenient to be so, because that meant I didn't have to be responsible to

anybody other than myself" (Miller 1). Since she was committed to being an atheist and

not believing in God, she was allowed to be selfish and only think of herself. The fact

that we want justice is a great proof of God's hand in morality. "Heather Mac Donald

disparages as 'wishful thinking' the idea that 'our moral sense and our passion for justice'

are 'faint echoes of a far more perfect morality and justice above.' Yet they are certainly

faint echoes of something. Our passion for justice burns so much hotter when we feel that

justice is on our side than when we don't" (Price 2). This quote shows the idea that our

sense of morality and justice must have come from somewhere, and there must have been

someone that set up that moral standard in the first place. If no one set up a moral

standard at the beginning of time, everyone would live by his or her own ideas of right or

wrong, and there would be no such thing as a moral standard. "Moral law, which seems

to be universal to humankind, calls us, on a regular basis, to do things that are not

consistent with the idea that our only purpose is to propagate our own DNA" (Miller 2).

This statement shows that we are not only looking out for ourselves, and there is something in us that makes us want to be selfless at times. If there were no God, then it would make sense for us to only care about our own well being, but since that is not always the case, God is a very reasonable explanation for this phenomenon.

Morality is such a great argument for the existence of God, that it needs another paragraph to truly do the arguments justice. "Our moral sense so often proves conveniently adjustable. Mac Donald's faith in these as human traits is quaint, especially after the 20th century. One could argue that, in such and such struggle, this side's moral sense was right and that side's was wrong. But that would be exactly to invoke a 'more perfect morality and justice' by which to judge the others" (Price 3). Someone, and not just anyone, must have thought up this "more perfect morality and justice". This shows that there must have been someone or something to create this perfect morality in the beginning of time to have it as a guideline for all of mankind. "Mac Donald accuses God of injustice in permitting undeserved suffering and death, as if these were the ultimate evil. At first that premise sounds plausible. Yet the more a fireman exposes himself to suffering and death, the less he deserves to undergo them. If undeserved suffering and death were the greatest evil, his first duty would be to protect himself, and it would be immoral for him to risk suffering and death for the sake of anyone more deserving of them than he. Removing God from the equation does not eliminate the need for paradox" (Price 3). The very fact of accusing God of injustice is showing that there must be a God. Why would anyone ever be disappointed with how life went, if there was no creator deciding how it went? If there were no God, no one would have reason to get disappointed about anything, because frankly, with no creator, whom can you blame for the bad things that happen in life? To sum it all up, "In my thinking (not just mine, of course, but influenced by C.S. Lewis, John Wesley, Plato, Boethius, Rodney Stark, Michel Borg, Bible Review magazine, the retired pastors at the Methodist church I attend, etc.), God's will is always for the good, for salvation and redemption for all. His will is only for healing, for life, for beauty, etc.--for every good thing" (Price 2). God is a completely good being, which gives a perfect explanation of why there is a widely accepted 'good and bad' on many issues. God put those morals in us when He created us, and that is the reason why the moral standard is so universal.

Many people believe that science and the belief in God are contradictory, but the fact is, there are numerous scientists that believe that God perfectly explains science. "Belief in God can be an entirely rational choice, and the principles of faith are, in fact, complementary with the principles of science" (Miller 1). The principles of faith are not contradictory with the truths of science, but rather complementary. Although some might say that belief in God makes you a man of faith rather than a man of science, the existence of God tends to clear up some issues that we already have with science and makes science complete in a sense. "When we look at the universe, when we look at the Earth, we don't know how to deal with all of the probabilities exactly, but we see it looks like it was set up so that life could happen, and where you see that setup, that fine-tuning, that's an argument for there being a designer who set it up and tuned it to do that" (Zweerink). Basically, with all of the specifications of Earth, there is no explanation for why Earth was formed the way it was. Other than an intelligent mind that fine-tuned the Earth to be that exact way, there isn't a very strong argument for any other reason that the earth would be like it is. Not only on Earth, but also, "it doesn't look like the conditions in which the moon is created is very common, it seems fine-tuned, and where you have fine-tuning, that's indicative of design, if you will, or an intelligent designer" (Zweerink).

These arguments for the specifications of the world as we know could only point to a

designer, and that designer is likely to be God as He is described.

The laws of physics that we have figured out are extremely complex, and there is

absolutely no rational way that they should have been so intricately designed by random.

"It's simply incoherent to claim that a universe of pure matter—with no purpose, no

intellect, no consciousness, no will whatsoever—can give rise to conscious, thinking,

willing beings" (Cartwright 3). The idea that nothing gave birth to something is

completely illogical, and could not possibly be true. In this way, it is logical to believe in

a biblical God, who has been hear since even before the beginning of time, and through

Him all things were made. "If you were to change the laws of physics, you end up with a

universe that doesn't have any hydrogen in it, or there's no oxygen, or no carbon. Well if

you've got a universe with no carbon, oxygen, or hydrogen, you don't have life"

(Zweerink). Everything that we take for granted on earth is what keeps us alive, and, if

anything changed, even something quite small, it could mean the end of humanity as we

know it. "Flew admitted that DNA shows that 'intelligence must have been involved in

getting these extraordinarily diverse elements together' and that he was now persuaded

that 'it is simply out of the question that the first living matter evolved out of dead matter

and then developed into an extraordinary, complicated creature'" (Cartwright 2). There is

no possible way that intelligent design was not involved with the creation of our world,

and the odds that our world was intricately formed by chance are astronomical.

When looking at the amazing philosophers and scientists who came up with some

of the most groundbreaking ideas generation after generation, we see that these geniuses believed in God and believed that God was essential for science. "As a Christian, I ask any searcher to examine the evidence for the truth of the Christian faith commonly advanced by the best Christian minds in generation after generation. From Augustine and Aquinas to Paul Tillich and Reinhold Niebuhr, through writers such as John Henry Newman, C.S. Lewis, G.K. Chesterton, Arnold Lunn, and Romano Guardini in more recent times, these evidences are steadily advanced, for those who seek them. The evidence is public and accessible to all, not simply private and individual. It is the witness of a public visible community, not merely subjective" (Novak 3). The evidence for the existence of God is laid out for everyone to see, and all you must do is search for it. So many scientists will completely ignore any case for the existence of God without looking at it, although if they did, they would most likely come to the same conclusion as many other scientists who had strong beliefs in God, and believed that God was crucial for science to work. The fact is that "most of the pioneers of modern science, including Einstein, were intuitively sound ontologists who recognized that the laws of nature can't be explained without an intelligent mind" (Cartwright 3). These brilliant scientists believed that there were some laws of nature that could not possibly be explained without the presence of an intelligent designer. These pioneers of science believed that there were some things the science just could not possibly explain, and in those moments, they turned to God as the answer. God, to them, was the completion of science, as what could not be explained by science, could be explained by the existence of God. "As Augustine realized, Plato's forms needed to be located somewhere, and the mind of God was the natural place to put them. Thus Augustine could argue that, since any successful science requires the existence of forms, there must be a God to eternally think them. No God, no science" (Clayton 1). Every new discovery in science is proof that there is someone that is constantly thinking them, and allowing humans to discover His masterpiece of the Earth. If we haven't figured out everything about the Earth yet, there is no way that the intricate laws of Earth were created randomly and with no purpose in mind.

The existence of God is not only allowed within the confines of science, but is actually essential for the very laws of science to make sense. "From Aristotle to (roughly) Galileo, 'to do science' meant to discover the four causes of a thing. The forms or 'formal causes' require a divine mind in which they can be located. Assuming that matter, or the material cause of a thing, is not eternal, it must be created--and by God, of course. Efficient causes-the sculptor who transforms a block of marble into a statue of Athena-- exist as separate from God; but since they are contingent, they too require God as their ultimate cause. The final cause or goal toward which everything develops is God, for God must be the one who brings about the final outcome of the earthly process in accordance with the divine aims. Again, it seemed, if there's no God, there's no science" (Clayton 2). There are numerous things that have been created, and the very fact that they have been created had to have been allowed by God, the creator of the universe. "Newton's laws seemed to account for the interactions of all bodies in the universe. Yet, as Newton realized, applying these laws required an ultimate, unchanging framework of 'absolute space' and 'absolute time' within which bodies moved. This framework could be located only within God as the eternal object of God's thought--or at least it could exist only with the concurrence of God's will and as a reflection of the divine nature. So Newton's laws, the greatest insight in the history of physics, appeared to communicate something of the nature of God" (Clayton 2). Newton's laws had to be based on the premise of absolute, unchanging space and time. These premises are not likely to remain the same without a creator creating them to do so. "Do you know how long it would take a supercomputer to perform the calculations involved in the reproduction of even one protein? Trillions and trillions of years" (Cartwright 4). The complexity of even one protein is so great that in order for it to work, there would be trillions of years to create something that could behave like that. Of course, an eternal God would find no problem with that.

One of the most obvious proofs that God is real is the fact that people can feel Him. "I do believe in the goodness of God, and I do believe that he knows better than I do. God sometimes says yes, God sometimes says no and God sometimes says wait. I've had to learn the difference between no and not yet. The issue here really does come down to surrender" (Meacham 2). God is present in every aspect of our lives, and people actually find answers to their prayers in their daily lives, whether it's answers they want or not. Many things that happen as a result of prayer cannot be explained in any way other than some being who controls the universe answering that prayer. "One of the great evidences of God is answered prayer. I have a friend, a Canadian friend, who has an immigration issue. He's an intern at this church, and so I said, 'God, I need you to help me with this,' as I went out for my evening walk. As I was walking I met a woman. She said, 'I'm an immigration attorney; I'd be happy to take this case.' Now, if that happened once in my life I'd say, 'That is a coincidence.' If it happened tens of thousands of times, that is not a coincidence" (Meacham 2). When he prayed about his friend, God sent a woman who could provide him with exactly what he needed, exactly when he needed it. There is no way that incidents like these can be shrugged off as coincidences. "Yet in that one same instant, God's eternal vision sees our prayers as part of the texture of events that unfolds itself in time. For us, all is sequential. For him, all is simultaneous. He wills the whole all at once. He understands it all, and he wills it all. He sees it as good, and he loves it" (Novak 5). It might be hard to understand how God answers prayers, but the reason for that is quite simple: God is not meant to be fully understood. He lives without being confined by time, and set in motion prayers to be answered before they are even prayed.

Although God Himself cannot be seen, the works that He does throughout the world and throughout our lives is clear. "There is a difference between a proof and a case. While a proof can be laid out and argued over with some movement toward rationality, a case tends to speak beyond the merely intellectual. It speaks to experiences, to emotions, to those unarticulated whispers resting just behind your right ear. And while many good cases are built on sturdy proof, some are relegated to the abyss between reason and intuition. Stirring up sediments of dismissed reflections, these cases challenge us to explore new pathways into territories we might otherwise have sealed off" (Hubele 3). There are many things that we believe that do not have completely solid proof in them, but we still believe them. The case for the existence of God is best proven through experiences and emotions, rather than the physical properties of proof. "I see the fingerprints of God everywhere. I see them in culture. I see them in law. I see them in literature. I see them in nature. I see them in my own life. Trying to understand where God came from is like an ant trying to understand the Internet. Even the most brilliant scientist would agree that we only know a fraction of a percent of the knowledge of the universe" (Meacham 1). God is so complex that there is no way that we can grasp the entirety of His being, but this actually gives proof to the fact that an infinitely complex

God would create an infinitely complex universe. If it was easy to understand God, it would be hard to believe that an understandable God could create a completely unable to be understood universe. "It is a category mistake to hold that God 'foresees' future events. In fact, and here the conception is philosophical, not based on Christian data: God dwells in a simultaneous present. Past, present, and future are all present to him in one vision. He sees the whole world of Time and all of this creation in one instant. He wills it all into being, and sustains it in being. Since by contrast we are in time, we must speak of past, present, and future. God is not bound by that constraint" (Novak 5). The complexity of God makes it easier to understand the complexity of His ways. When something completely out of the ordinary occurs, a miracle, it is logical to attribute the unexplainable instance to an unexplainable God.

The only way that we can show sacrificial love is if we have an example of this, and the best example unconditional love is God's love for us. "The problem of pain and suffering does not disappear, but the problem of love does. We may still have to face challenges from friends and from life itself, but at least now we face them from within this case. And who knows? Love just may be the strongest case we have" (Hubele 3). When bad things happen to people we love, we do everything we can to help them. Now some may say that God is the one that brought upon those circumstances, but maybe He is giving us a chance to show love towards someone, a love that He invented in the first place. "St. John the Evangelist wields his one-word description as a case. And the best I can do in the face of suffering is to turn back to that beautiful and enigmatic case: God is love. It is only when I ask challenging questions and let them bounce off that particular description of God that I can begin to reach a glimmer of understanding" (Hubele 3).

When bad things happen, we might not see the love of God through it, but unconditional love was created by God, so who are we to say what unconditional love is? We can get glimpses of unconditional love when going through hard times and someone decides to love us, but the Son of God gave that first example of unconditional love when He died on the cross. "Yet a humanity-saving, selfless love -- even between strangers -- does exist in our world. How is that? Knowing the worst we are capable of whether genocidal camps or weapons of mass destruction, we should not ask, How can God watch so much pain, and stand by? but rather, Why is that we don't just stand by? What is it inside us that makes us denounce pain and suffering and work to prevent and overcome it? There is selflessness in such empathy. It is a selflessness that does not come from the same creative place within humanity that dreamed up poison gas, torture or ways to dehumanize the poor. Knowing the worst humanity is capable of, we must admit that such uncharacteristic selflessness seems to come from something other than human. Something apart, beyond. Call it what you will. I call it God" (Hubele 3). When bad things happen to other people, why is it that people gather together to help them? It is best explained by how we were created by a loving God who put a tendency of sacrificial love inside of us.

  In conclusion, the existence of God is not denied by science, but is rather accepted by many highly esteemed scientists and theologians. God is not a made up answer to some of science's questions, but a completely logical explanation to everything we know about science. The concrete evidence brought forth in this paper shows the many reasons why it is probable that a god does exist. From the complex physical aspects of everything on earth and in space to the unexplainable moral compass and sacrificial love that humans show, all things point to the existence of a god who created it all. The God of the Bible is a perfect explanation for many of the world's mysteries, and because of that, it is completely logical to believe in Him.

Works Cited

Cartwright, Gary. "Me And Him." Texas Monthly 33.5 (2005): 88-101. Readers'
    Guide Full Text Mega (H.W. Wilson). Web. 23 Feb. 2016.

Clayton, Philip. "Emerging God." Christian Century 121.1 (2004): 26-30. Readers'
    Guide Full Text Mega (H.W. Wilson). Web. 23 Feb. 2016.

Grove, Phillip Editor in Chief. Webster's Third New International Dictionary.
    Springfield, Mass: Merriam-Webster, 2002. Print.

Hubele, M. M. "Looking For Love." America 201.8 (2009): 20-21. Readers' Guide
    Full Text Mega (H.W. Wilson). Web. 23 Feb. 2016.

Meacham, Jon. "The God Debate." Newsweek 149.15 (2007): 58-63. Readers' Guide
    Full Text Mega (H.W. Wilson). Web. 23 Feb. 2016.

Miller, David Ian. "Francis S. Collins." Progressive Christian (19347316) 181.2
    (2007): 18-19. Readers' Guide Full Text Mega (H.W. Wilson). Web. 3 Mar.
    2016.

Novak, Michael. "To An Atheist Friend: Conservatives, Heather Mac Donald And
    Disagreements About God." American Spectator 39.9 (2006): 14-21.
    Readers' Guide Full Text Mega (H.W. Wilson). Web. 23 Feb. 2016.

Price, Laurie. "God and Man." American Spectator 40.2   (2007): 8. Readers' Guide
    Full Text Mega (H.W. Wilson). Web. 3 Mar. 2016.

Zweerink, Jeffrey. Personal Interview. 3 Mar. 2016

YOUR KNOWLEDGE HAS VALUE

- We will publish your bachelor's and master's thesis, essays and papers

- Your own eBook and book - sold worldwide in all relevant shops

- Earn money with each sale

Upload your text at www.GRIN.com
and publish for free